365 DAYS

★ ★ ★ ★ ★ ★ ★ **OF** ★ ★ ★ ★ ★ ★ ★

PRAYER

365 DAYS OF PRAYER

Summersdale Publishers Ltd
46 West Street
Chichester
West Sussex
PO19 1RP
UK

www.summersdale.com

Printed and bound in the Czech Republic

ISBN: 978-1-84953-656-1

Substantial discounts on bulk quantities of Summersdale books are available to corporations, professional associations and other organisations. For details contact Nicky Douglas by telephone: +44 (0) 1243 756902, fax: +44 (0) 1243 786300 or email: nicky@summersdale.com.

365 DAYS OF PRAYER

Victoria Lorenzato

summersdale

For my daughters, Emma & Amy, and my godsons, Charley & Nathan; may you know God's love all the days of your life.

To.....Tanya...

From......Sue....x.......................................

JANUARY

1

New Year's Day: As you begin this New Year, commit to making time each day for a short period of prayer and reflection. Today, make time to thank God for the blessings of the year that has passed.

2 *A prayer for resolutions*

Lord, I call on you for the strength and determination to keep my resolutions so that I might grow to know myself and your plan for my life. Amen.

Take time today to walk outside and appreciate the beauty of God's winter creation, from the frost patterns on windowpanes to your warm breath on the cold air.

 Try to abandon preconceptions about prayer. Your own journey with God is as unique as you are.

 A prayer for wisdom
God, I pray today for the gift of wisdom that I might better serve you and others with the choices that I make. Amen.

 Consider lighting a candle as a focus for your prayer.

Prayer is where the action is.

John Wesley

Prayer is an act of love, words are not needed.

St Teresa of Ávila

A prayer to help with prayer
Lord, it can be difficult to know what to say sometimes. Guide my heart and mind to find the right words for you today. Amen.

 The word 'prayer' has its roots in the Latin word *precarius*, which means to entreat or to ask in earnest. What do you ask in earnest from God today?

 A prayer for compassion
God, open my eyes to see your face in all whom I encounter today. Fill me with compassion for those in need. Amen.

Prayers don't need to be lengthy. A short prayer that has your undivided attention can be squeezed into the busiest of days.

 A prayer for gifts
Today I thank you, Lord, for the unique talents you have given to me. Help me to make the best use of these talents without boasting about or wasting them. Amen.

 A prayer for peace
Create in me, O Lord, a peace-loving nature. Help me to understand that peace in our world begins with peace in my life. Amen.

15 If you find yourself in a stressful situation, stop and take a deep breath and call on God's help.

 16 You don't have to kneel or stand to pray. You can pray in your favourite armchair or at the kitchen sink. Where are you most comfortable?

 17 *A prayer for generosity*
Help me today, Lord, to have a generous spirit, recognising that I often have more than I need. Amen.

 18 Commit to a feeling of tranquillity before sleep each night; banish technology from your bedroom.

Martin Luther King Day: Remember in thanksgiving and prayer today those who work tirelessly for a world free from prejudice and discrimination.

 God knows your needs before you do, but asking helps your own clarity and sense of purpose.

 Keep in mind today those who are gifted artists, and thank God for your own artistic talents. Think of your favourite piece of art and how it might aid your prayer today.

Use an image of a heart as your prayer focus today. Are you living life as a wholehearted person? Are you open-hearted? Hard-hearted? Half-hearted?

 A prayer for courage
In times of fear, remind me, O Lord, that with you nothing is impossible. Amen.

 Think of three things each evening that you are grateful for. This is a great habit to improve your perspective on life!

 Prayer is an integral part of all of the major world faiths; today consider your prayer joining with the prayers of others throughout the world.

I am walking proof of the power of prayer.

Fabrice Muamba

Our prayers should be
for blessings in general,
for God knows best
what is good for us.

Anonymous

28 For prayer ideas on the go, consider downloading a 'prayer-a-day' app for your smartphone or tablet.

 29 *A prayer for dignity and respect*
We are all made in your image and likeness, Lord; grant that all people experience the respect and dignity your creation deserves. Amen.

 30 Don't be afraid to pray as children do; keep it simple and speak from the heart.

 31 Remember today that God has the power to make all things new.

FEBRUARY

A February prayer
Creator God, when I struggle on cold winter mornings, help me to remember the promise of new beginnings that spring will bring. Amen.

Try using a Bible or other holy book as a source of inspiration for your prayer. Choose a passage at random and reflect on its meaning for you today.

Remember that praying for people in need is a way of supporting them.

FEBRUARY

 A prayer for those suffering from cancer
On World Cancer Day, I pray for all of those affected by cancer, for those who are suffering and their families, for their doctors and nurses, and for those who are working for a cure. Amen.

5 Consider everyone you meet as a child of God. It might just help you feel more tolerant!

UNICEF Day for Change: Focus on the theme of change for your prayer today. What change would you like to see in your life? What change does the world most need?

A prayer for forgiveness
When I feel the burden of wrongdoing,
help me to keep in mind that no negative
action of mine is stronger than the
positive power of your love for me. Amen.

 If you are struggling to forgive someone,
remember that forgiveness is choosing
to let go of the anger and upset; hand
it over to God and choose to move on.

 A prayer for music
It has been said that he who sings prays
twice. Today, Lord, I thank you for the
gift of music and its influence in my
life. Amen.

A prayer for letting go of the past
When I feel regret about moments in my past, help me to remember that these have shaped the person that I am today. Amen.

 Get creative! If writing your prayers doesn't suit you, why not sketch or paint your message to God today?

 A prayer for creativity
Help me to remember, Lord, that my creativity is a gift from you. Remove my fear of imperfection and allow me to embrace the richness and joy of self-expression. Amen.

FEBRUARY

 13 *A prayer for those preparing for marriage*
Lord, I ask you to be with those who
begin their lifetime journey together in
the coming months. Sustain their love
for one another and strengthen them
in times of challenge. Amen.

 14

Valentine's Day: To love and be loved
is a fundamental human need. Today
pray for all of the people who have
taught you about love in your life.
Remember, too, those who face today
feeling unloved.

 15 Thank God for any kindnesses shown
to you today. Ask God to help you share
this with others tomorrow.

And what is God? Supreme happiness. That is all.

St Madeleine Sophie Barat

For where your
treasure is, there your
heart will be also.

Matthew's Gospel 6:21

A prayer for those grieving
Today I place into your care those who are grieving the loss of a loved one. When no words may comfort them, may they feel your loving presence. Amen.

 A prayer for decision making
For the times when I find several paths ahead of me, I ask for your guidance to make the right choice and the wisdom to accept your plan for me. Amen.

 A prayer for fair trade
Help me to make wise choices to support the campaign for fair trade. The goodness of your creation should be shared fairly throughout the world. Amen.

Think of God as a listening friend who knows you completely. What advice would such a person offer you?

 A prayer for the gift of language and communication
You have granted us, Lord, the wonderful gift of language. In all of my communications today, may I choose the kindest words and most thoughtful expressions. Amen.

 A prayer for careful thought
For the times when I rush to respond to a situation that challenges me, Lord, help me to pause and seek a response from both my head and my heart. Amen.

Omnia vincit Amor.
(Love conquers all.)

Virgil

Life can only be understood backwards; but it must be lived forwards.

Søren Kierkegaard

26 Whether you choose Gregorian chant or birdsong, find music that calms you as an aid to your prayer today.

 27 If you find it hard to relax before meditation, find a comfortable position and consciously tense and relax muscle groups to let go of any stress.

 28 Daily prayer will help you to develop a greater awareness of each individual moment in your life.

 29 Consider this extra day as a gift from God, and show your appreciation with an act of kindness for a stranger, or an extended time of quiet prayer.

MARCH

A March prayer

When I see the first spring flowers and feel the first rays of warm sunshine, help me to shake off the lethargy of winter and find more energy and a renewed vigour for life. Amen.

Consider writing a letter to God. You may choose to keep your letters to reflect upon at a later date or you may wish to tear them up and throw them away as a symbol of handing over your worries to God.

Often the answer to our prayer is already with us. The process of prayer helps us to understand and accept this answer.

 As Jesus said, 'Love your enemies.' It's easy to pray for loved ones; try a real challenge today and ask God's blessing upon those with whom you struggle.

 A prayer for writers
I thank you, Lord, for the gift of writing and the joy brought by reading. I pray that all people throughout the world will have access to the essential skills of literacy. Amen.

Pray, and let God worry.

Martin Luther

Pray to catch the bus and then run as fast as you can.

Julia Cameron

MARCH

International Women's Day: Take time today to thank God for the women in your life and ask for God's help for women living with inequality and discrimination.

 Collective worship can be very powerful. Consider finding out about groups and events at your local place of worship.

 You are never too young to have prayer in your life. If you are a new parent, begin your baby's lifelong journey with God by sharing a quiet moment of prayer beside their crib each night.

A prayer for sport
Lord, today I thank you for sport, and those women and men who dedicate their lives to surpassing expectations. May I apply their determination and self-belief in my own life. Amen.

 A morning prayer
God of the morning, give me the grace to rise today filled with energy, joy and a willingness to see your goodness in every person that I meet. Amen.

 Prayer intentions can sometimes read like a child's Christmas list. Don't forget to say thank you as well as please!

MARCH

 A prayer for new beginnings
For the times when I face the start of a
new venture, I ask your blessing, Lord.
Help me to recognise your guiding hand
in the kindness and support of others.
Amen.

 Pray today for those who are involved
in mothering. Remember your mother,
your grandmothers and women
everywhere preparing for motherhood.
If you are a mother, thank God for the
remarkable gift of parenting and ask God
for support when facing the challenges
that come with being a mother.

To be friends with God means to pray with simplicity, like children talking to their parents.

Pope Francis

Let nothing perturb you,
nothing frighten you. All
things pass. God does
not change. Patience
achieves everything.

St Teresa of Ávila

A bedtime prayer
I thank you, Lord, for the many blessings of today. I place into your hands those situations which trouble me and ask for your peace this night and always. Amen.

 A prayer for world leaders
God of compassion, I pray today for those in authority throughout the world. Guide them to lead with compassion, truth and justice for all peoples. Amen.

 Try this breathing exercise to help you pray: as you draw in a deep breath think, 'God be with me,' and as you exhale slowly, 'all through this day.' Repeat several times to aid relaxation.

MARCH

World Poetry Day: Find a favourite poem as your focus for prayer. Consider trying to express your prayer today as a poem.

A prayer for clean water

I pray for those in the world without access to clean water. May I support those working for the provision of this basic need, whilst being mindful of its value. Amen.

Keep in mind the wonder of the season of spring. Try to spend some time outside, using all of your senses, and thanking God for the beauty of his creation.

MARCH

 A prayer for trusting God's plan
Lord, I ask you to increase my trust in your plan for my life. Help me to turn to you when I am seeking answers, knowing that you hold the key to my happiness. Amen.

 Seek God's grace today. Where is God working in your life?

 When you wake, engage in some whole-body stretches and call to mind in prayer those who need God's help today.

 Are you a fan of Twitter? What would your tweet to God say today? Remember you only have 140 characters!

MARCH

Earth Hour: As you spend an hour reducing your energy consumption today, pray for greater awareness of the needs of our world and the environment.

 As the clocks go forward this month, make the most of the extra daylight by taking your prayer outside.

 Conflict about religion often stems from ignorance. Commit to being more open-minded about the faiths of others.

 Learn to see God's face and hear God's voice in the words and actions of others.

APRIL

April Fool's Day: Take time today to thank God for the gift of laughter in our lives. It can be easy to take ourselves far too seriously!

An April prayer
As I see signs of new life around me, help me to remember your loving care for all of creation and your ability to make all things new. Amen.

If you are feeling anger or despair, hand those feelings over to God.

All shall be well, and
all shall be well, and
all manner of things
shall be well.

Julian of Norwich

Don't pray when it rains if you don't pray when the sun shines.

Leroy 'Satchel' Paige

APRIL

 A prayer for hope after despair
Carry me through those moments when I feel all is lost. Help me, Lord, to remember that even in my darkest times there is hope of joy in the days to come. Amen.

World Health Day: Thank God today for your health and pray for greater equality in access to healthcare throughout the world.

 A prayer for self-confidence
For the times when I am the last person to believe what I am capable of, gently guide me to know my value and worth. Amen.

9 Use all of your senses when you pray. Choose a scented candle or a favourite piece of music as a focus for prayer.

 10 Pray today for your closest friend or companion. Thank God for the gift of their love and support in your life.

 11 *A prayer for respect for the earth's resources* God of all creation, may I never take the earth's gifts for granted. I pray for those who work to protect the planet and resolve to live in a way that sustains its resources. Amen.

APRIL

 A prayer for affirming others
God of love, help me always to seek the goodness in others and take the time to share the joy and delight that knowing them brings to my life. Amen.

 Pay greater attention to your journey to work or college today. Do you pass a school or a hospital? A police station or a church? Pray for those within these places who need God's help.

 Lose your shoes today! Many faith traditions pray with bare feet; not only can this be humbling, it gives a sense of feeling more grounded as you pray.

A prayer for culture

I pray today for a greater understanding and appreciation of my cultural heritage. Help me to recognise our common membership of a global family and to embrace what can be learned from other cultures. Amen.

 If you feel short of time, make prayer a part of your daily routine. Why not pray each time you make a hot drink or during the same part of your commute each day?

 Plant a seed; the nurture and care of a living thing will develop in you a deeper appreciation for creation as you watch it grow.

A prayer for resisting negativity
For the times when it seems easier to expect the worst, remind me, Lord, of all that is possible with true faith in you. Amen.

 If you have young children in your life, simply ask them to name who they wish to pray for each night before bedtime.

 Hold in your prayers today all of those who are sick and in need of healing. Ask God to comfort them and those who provide their care.

It's easy to obsess over a miraculous solution to our problems; don't overlook the everyday transformations happening around you.

 A prayer for dreams
I place into your hands today, O Lord, my wildest dreams and desires. Help me to believe in my potential to make them a reality, one small step at a time. Amen.

 Value silence; aim for a day without any background noise and listen to what God might be trying to say to you.

Prayer is a path where there is none.

Noah ben Shea

Never forget the three powerful resources you always have available to you: love, prayer, and forgiveness.

H. Jackson Brown, Jr

A prayer for finding the right words
For the times when I struggle to know what to say, help me to know when being present is enough and when my actions will provide the best support for a person in need. Amen.

 Find a thing of beauty today and thank God for it. If it is the work of human hands, thank God for the talents given to make it.

 Consider keeping a prayer journal. Expressive writing can have a positive impact on stress levels, health and well-being.

Thank God today for the gifts of movement and dance. Many faith traditions use these gifts as a form of prayer; this may be an activity that you would enjoy.

 A prayer for doctors
I pray today, Lord, for doctors throughout the world who are charged with the challenge and privilege of caring for the sick. Bless them with the patience and strength to support them in their daily challenges. Amen.

MAY

1

May Day: Ancient May Day festivals traditionally included a celebration of the start of summer and, in some cases, were graced by Flora, the Roman goddess of flowers. Find time today for a few moments outside to appreciate the changing seasons and the beauty of flowers.

2 If you are a fan of social media, there are many shared prayer groups available on Facebook and Twitter offering a sense of community across the world.

Prayer is prehistoric; anthropologists have discovered evidence of community-based symbolic acts from 35,000 years ago during a period in human development known as 'The Great Leap Forward'.

 Forgive yourself. Let it go. Write it down and offer it to God.

 A prayer for midwives
I pray today, Lord, for women and men who help to bring new life into the world. Bless them and the sanctity of their work and watch over all those who become parents today. Amen.

A prayer for openness to joy
Lord, help me this day and always to seek the moments of joy and happiness that can be so easily overlooked when I am busy. Amen.

 Don't be afraid to take young children into places of worship; they are the future, after all! Many places hold special family services or offer prayer resources to keep them occupied.

 A prayer for the Red Cross and Red Crescent
I ask your blessing, Lord, for organisations which provide support in areas affected by conflict and natural disaster. Watch over those who risk their lives for those in need. Amen.

If you are planning a holiday, explore whether a visit to a pilgrimage site is possible. Witnessing pilgrims congregating at a sacred site can be a powerful affirmation of faith.

 A prayer for farmers
For all of those who rely on the land for their income and whose labour provides nourishment, I ask your blessing, Lord. Amen.

 The word *Amen* means 'so be it' in Hebrew and is used in Christianity, Judaism and Islam; prayer and trust – that God hears our prayers – go hand in hand.

Nurses' Day: Keep in mind today nurses who care for the vulnerable and sick. If you know a nurse, make a point of thanking them for their vocation today.

 A prayer for exams

God, I remember today anyone who is preparing for exams. Help them to achieve their potential, reflecting the gifts that you have bestowed upon them. Amen.

 Prayer is a conversation with God. Don't be afraid to stop and listen to God's response once in a while.

International Day of Families: Thank God for the support of families and let your family know that you are praying for them today.

A prayer for forgiveness
I ask your forgiveness, Lord, for the times when I am burdened with guilt for my mistakes, and your support in my commitment to avoid repeating them. Amen.

Use your hands as a focus for prayer today. How have you used them recently? To console and embrace or to judge and dismiss?

Don't pray for lighter burdens but for stronger backs.

Oscar Wilde

Courage is fear that has said its prayers.

Dorothy Bernard

Do you share your birthday with a saint or holy person? Research their life and see how it might influence your own faith.

 The only prerequisite for prayer is that you come as you are.

 Recognising the need for help is a sign of strength, not weakness; keep this in mind as you pray for yourself today.

 A prayer for open-mindedness
When I feel I know best before listening to others, help me, Lord, to have an open mind, recognising that there is always more that I can learn. Amen.

Open yourself in prayer to God. Try holding your hands flat with your palms facing upwards to represent an openness to receive God's wisdom for you today.

 Be flexible in your prayer time. Some days you may want to give more time to prayer; be sure to give yourself the time that you need to express yourself.

 As a focus for your prayer today, think of those who live nearest to you. Commit to showing them small acts of kindness in the coming weeks.

Be still, and know that I am God.

Psalm 46:10

Let silence take you to the core of life.

Rumi

Visiting a place of worship from a different faith tradition can be a great source of awe and wonder. Consider arranging a visit and gaining a new perspective on faith.

 A prayer for the lonely
Lord, I place into your loving care those who feel alone today. Open my eyes to see those in need of comfort or support around me. Amen.

 God is a mystery. Just like a knot, sometimes the more we try to unravel this mystery, the more difficult God is to grasp. Try not to grasp but to experience God's presence without question.

JUNE

 At this point in the year, take a few moments to reflect upon your prayer journey. Thank God for the blessings of this journey and ask for help where it is needed.

 Many faith traditions use handheld objects, such as prayer beads, to aid focus whilst praying. If you are a tactile person, consider how this might help you.

3 Don't worry if you feel you have nothing to say to God today. Perhaps this is the time for listening instead.

 4 Prayer is only part of the solution; don't forget the need for action.

 5 *A prayer for the environment*
Lord, I pray that humanity appreciates the gift of our world and tirelessly seeks to protect it for future generations. Amen.

 6 *A prayer for the Armed Forces*
God of peace, I ask your blessing upon all of those who risk their lives to promote and protect peace in our world. Amen.

A prayer for regret
Help me today, Lord, to recognise the energy wasted in regret. Help me to focus instead on making good choices in the future. Amen.

World Oceans Day: On World Oceans Day, focus your prayer today on those who live and work on the seas.

 A prayer for the anxious
God of calm and quiet, lessen the worries of those with troubled minds today. Amen.

What wings are to a bird, and sails to a ship, so is prayer to the soul.

Corrie ten Boom

To live by faith means to put our lives in the hands of God, especially in our most difficult moments.

Pope Francis

JUNE

Anne Frank Day: Today, reflect on and pray for young people who take great risks and show courage in the face of adversity.

 If you are going through a difficult time, ask yourself how this experience might help you grow.

 We are used to multitasking and perpetual noise. Why not research opportunities for a day or more of silent retreat?

 No matter how far you find yourself from home, a visit to a place of worship can be a great source of comfort and familiarity.

Praying with young children before bedtime makes for a calm end to the day. Encourage them to name a person they want to thank God for or someone who might need God's help.

 If you feel overwhelmed today, walk outside and look up. A cloudless sky or a starry night are both humbling reminders of our part in the bigger picture.

 Consider adopting a famous saying or way of life of a holy person or saint. How might this change the way that you approach today?

A prayer for the emergency services
For the courage and compassion of those who work in the emergency services, I ask for your blessing and protection, Lord. Amen.

World Refugee Day: Remember all those who are forced to leave their homes in your prayer today. Commit to developing a deeper sense of compassion for their suffering.

 A prayer for fathers
God, who is called Father, I thank you for fathers everywhere. Watch over and guide all new fathers and all those who act as a father to others. Amen.

JUNE

 A prayer for listening
Help me, Lord, to really listen to what others are saying to me today, rather than focusing on what I think I hear. Amen.

 A prayer for summer
As the days are at their longest, I thank you, Lord, for the summertime and the happiness the season brings. Amen.

 Don't obsess about clearing your mind whilst meditating. Rather than trying to ignore any persistent thoughts that come to mind, recognise that they might be significant to you and then choose to move on.

JUNE

 Reflect today upon any barriers preventing you from living a more prayer-filled life, and think about ways by which you can reduce or remove them.

 Consider placing an important photo or image on your desk as a catalyst to prayer in times of stress.

 Create a prayer jar; add intentions or names of family members or friends and choose a prayer focus each day.

 As you pray today, focus on the all-loving and all-knowing nature of God. Don't worry about finding the right words.

Prayers go up and blessings come down.

Yiddish proverb

Call on God, but row away from the rocks.

Indian proverb

JULY

 Keep in mind today those for whom this month signals the end of a year: students graduating from university, pupils finishing school and all of those who work in education.

 Many radio stations offer a 'Thought for the Day'. Consider tuning in and discerning what the message might mean for you today.

Faith in God is only half the story. The other half is faith in God's power to answer your prayers.

 Research and debate continues over the healing power of prayer; but, for people who pray, the comfort and help they experience is all too apparent.

 If you find yourself judging someone today, pray for compassion and a more open mind.

God gave us two ears and one mouth to be used in those proportions.

Irish proverb

If we could change
ourselves, the tendencies
in the world would
also change.

Gandhi

A prayer in remembrance
I hold in my prayers today all those who are suffering the loss of a loved one. I thank God for the life and love shared by those who now rest with God. Amen.

 Reflect on your uniqueness today; there is no one in the world exactly like you. Have you discovered God's purpose for you yet?

 If you or a loved one is daunted by a trip to hospital, consider contacting the hospital chaplain, who can arrange a bedside visit and prayer.

Does everything have to have a price? Pray for God's help in offering and accepting hospitality with no strings attached.

 A prayer for hope
God, help me to remember that to live a hopeful life is to believe in the power of good. Let me never lose a sense of optimism in my life. Amen.

 Where do you feel most at peace? Prayer can happen anywhere at any time.

Pray, hope and don't worry. Worry is useless. God is merciful and will hear your prayer.

St Padre Pio

We have to pray with our eyes on God, not on the difficulties.

Oswald Chambers

A prayer for saying goodbye
Help me, Lord, when I struggle to be parted from someone. When letting go is difficult, keep us both in your loving care. Amen.

 A prayer for learning
I ask your help, Lord, in seeing each new day as a learning opportunity. May I always remain open to new insights. Amen.

Mandela Day: Keep in mind today the remarkable legacy of Nelson Mandela. Ask God's help in seeking unconditional reconciliation where it is needed in your life.

Take time to watch the grass grow. Observe the world of nature today, even if it's only for five minutes during your lunch break.

 Many see prayer as a path to discernment. How does God influence the choices that you make?

 Rather than talking to God, spend five minutes listening today.

 Count your blessings, and you'll find more than you think.

Just like the radio, every now and then we need to retune to hear God's voice and eliminate the chatter.

 A prayer before meals
For this meal, and for the many ways that you nourish me, I thank you, Lord. Amen.

 If you find it difficult to clear your mind whilst meditating, imagine a blank sheet of paper in front of you.

 As you pray before you go to sleep tonight, visualise passing any unresolved situations over to God.

A prayer for the beauty of creation
Open my eyes, Lord, to the beauty of your world around me. Help me to recognise your divine order in all things. Amen.

 Religious music comes in as many forms and styles as secular music. Whether you favour opera or rap, explore some religious alternatives and learn to pray with both words and music as you listen.

 Take a moment today to reflect on how the world would be if God answered all prayers.

International Day of Friendship: Keep in mind today the friends who have travelled with you in your life's journey. Ask for God's blessing upon them, wherever they may be.

 A prayer for persistence

Though obstacles might hinder my progress, Lord, help me to persist with those tasks which matter most to me today. Amen.

AUGUST

  An August prayer

I am showered in blessings, but sometimes fail to see them. In this holiday month, I pray that I might take the time to pause, recharge and take stock of my life. Amen.

  Use a news story as a focus for your prayer today. In some situations it often feels as though all we have is prayer.

The words 'health' and 'holy' and 'whole' all come from the same word. What is the connection between these words in your own life?

 Unanswered prayers can cause great frustration. Rather than battling with what can seem like insurmountable obstacles, trust in God's plan for you.

 If you are struggling to keep a promise or resist a craving today, pause for a moment of prayer, asking God for strength and determination.

AUGUST

 A prayer for accepting God's plan
I want to know your plan for me, O Lord. Challenge me to trust you more each day as I try to live according to your will. Amen.

 You may think prayer to an all-knowing God is unnecessary, but it is often in the asking that the answers become apparent.

 We are conditioned to filter out the positive at times. Today, focus on the good that you hear and feel about yourself.

The root, the fountain, the mother of a thousand blessings.

St John Chrysostomon prayer

I have lived to thank God
that all my prayers have
not been answered.

Jean Ingelow

AUGUST

 Prayer helps develop self-awareness by giving you time to reflect upon what is truly important.

International Youth Day: Young people all over the world achieve the seemingly impossible every day. Strive to seek opportunities to affirm the young people in your life. If you are a young person, resolve to keep your youthful optimism as you journey toward adulthood.

 Today ask God's help in seeking what is right even when it is not what is popular.

A prayer for self-control
At times, Lord, my feelings get the better of me. Help me balance how I feel with how these feelings might affect those around me. Amen.

 A prayer for social justice
We have all been created in your image, Lord, as equals to one another. Help me strive to bring about social justice for all in every aspect of my life. Amen.

 Many places of worship have prayer boards or books where intentions can be written that will then be remembered by the community. Seek out this valuable resource during your next visit.

It is of great importance,
when we begin to
practise prayer, not to let
ourselves be frightened
by our own thoughts.

St Teresa of Ávila

Prayer does not change God, but it changes him who prays.

Søren Kierkegaard

AUGUST

World Humanitarian Day: Spend time reflecting upon how you view your place in the human race. Are you worthy of the title 'humanitarian'? What more could you do?

 Pray outside today. The Gospels recount more examples of Jesus praying outside than in temples or other buildings.

 A prayer not to turn a blind eye
Lord, when I face a situation that demands bravery and courage in defending another person, be with me in any discomfort I may feel. Amen.

AUGUST

 22 Ask God to ground you as you pray today; if you find yourself worrying about the past or the future, try wiggling your toes and remember the importance of now.

 23 Many faith traditions liken God's love to that of a parent. Hold this thought in mind as you pray today.

 24 *A prayer for those travelling*
My prayer today is for all those who are making journeys, whether for work or leisure. Lord, be with those who are anxious and grant patience to those who may otherwise fail to recognise the needs of their fellow travellers. Amen.

Don't think of prayer as a secret recipe but as a chance for dialogue with the head chef!

 Sometimes we can be so busy looking for the lightning bolt that we overlook the still small voice of God in the kind words of a family member or friend.

 Ask God to help you find the right path in life; but don't just sit there – keep moving!

 Communication is at the heart of any relationship; prayer strengthens your relationship with God.

There is no prayer you can imagine that is too great for the power of God.

 A prayer for sleep
I am in need of rest, Lord. Reach into my busy mind and heart and remove those obstacles that hinder my sleep tonight. Amen.

 Keep in mind today those who work for unity between religions, and pray for those who misuse their faith as a justification for conflict.

SEPTEMBER

 1 Keep in mind today all those involved in education: children beginning school, teachers and especially parents, the first educators of the young.

2 *A prayer for lifelong learning*
Help me to rise each day seeking out opportunities for new learning, recognising that education is a gift for life. Amen.

SEPTEMBER

 Today, thank God for the people that matter most in your life. Remember to take time to show them how much they mean to you.

 Sometimes there are no right words; there is only faith and silence. Offer a wordless prayer to God, who knows what is in your heart.

 Religion has always been a popular theme for artists. Visit an art gallery and notice any pieces which appeal to you. Take time to study and reflect on them as an act of prayer today.

SEPTEMBER

 A prayer for comfort
For the times when I feel distress, help me to find comfort in the knowledge of your loving presence. Amen.

 You may feel you don't have the answer to a particular question at the moment. As you pray today, ask yourself this: 'If I did know the answer, what might it be?'

International Literacy Day: As a focus for your prayer today, remember those throughout the world whose life chances are limited by a lack of literacy skills.

God speaks in the silence
of the heart. Listening is
the beginning of prayer.

Mother Teresa

Every Christian needs
a half-hour of prayer
each day, except when
he is busy, and then
he needs an hour.

St Francis De Sales

The tragic events of 11 September 2001 saw an increase in attendance at places of worship in New York City. Prayer can be a powerful and unifying force for a community in need.

 A prayer for clarity
I am listening, Lord, to so many voices every day. Help me to listen and seek the right choices in keeping with your plan for my life. Amen.

 Remember in prayer today grandmothers and grandfathers throughout the world. Find the time today to thank the grandparents in your life for all that they do.

A prayer for separated families
Lord, I ask you to be with those families who are unable to be together. May your love connect them despite the distance that separates them. Amen.

 A prayer for politics
I pray today that those who work in politics will recognise the voice of every individual and use their position of power with humility and compassion. Amen.

To clasp the hands in prayer is the beginning of an uprising against the disorder of the world.

Karl Barth

If you are what you should be, you will set the whole world on fire.

St Catherine of Siena

SEPTEMBER

 A prayer for letting go
For the times that I hold on to moments from the past and painful memories, I ask you, Lord, to remind me of the treasure of the present moment. Amen.

 It's a symptom of today's society to insist on taking action and expecting instant results. Make a conscious choice to slow down today and recognise when less action and more thought might be preferable.

 A prayer for the elderly
I ask you, Lord, to hold in your loving arms those in their later years. I thank you for their wisdom and ask that their experiences are always cherished. Amen.

SEPTEMBER

International Day of Peace: Focus your prayer today on peace in our world and resolve to live a more peace-filled life.

 Today, imagine your prayer for those in need as a light in the darkness.

 What are you looking at but not yet seeing?

 The next time you face a challenging person, ask God for the wisdom to see things from their perspective.

Pray today for help in trusting feelings as well as facts.

 If you are seeking peace in our world, begin by praying for peace in your home. Choose words and actions that promote peace in your relationships and see the positive impact this has on those around you.

 As your prayer life develops, reflect on how often you pray for yourself and others. Love of God, valuing yourself and being of service to others are all vital aspects of a prayer-filled life.

Today, approximately 370,000 babies will be born around the world. Hold them and their parents in your prayers today, that their lives will be filled with joy they will share with others.

 Whilst it can be difficult to say goodbye to summer and embrace autumn, remember that change is the catalyst for new growth.

 A prayer for love
Loving God, help me to recognise the gift of love in the actions of others and guide me to share this love with those I encounter today. Amen.

OCTOBER

 Try to get outside to pray today. Notice the colour of the changing leaves and thank God for the beauty of nature's circle of life.

 As you pray today, imagine substituting the weights in your life for balloons. What is dragging you down? What is lifting you up?

If you have been upset by someone's actions in recent days, pray today for understanding of their needs as well as your own.

 A prayer for the past
Lord, help me to recognise that my past, both painful and joyful, has shaped the person I am today. Amen.

World Teachers' Day: Take a moment of prayer today to remember your favourite teacher. Ask for God's blessing upon all of those charged with the privilege and the challenge of educating others.

A prayer for animals and those who care for them

I pray today that humankind will remember to respect the animal kingdom and the many riches that it has to share with us. Amen.

 Next time a friend or relative shares a burden with you, offer to remember them in your prayers. Regardless of their own faith journey, few will object to your kindness.

 'Treat others as you wish to be treated' is a principle seen in many faith traditions. Pray today for a greater capacity to care for others and for yourself.

Without faith, nothing is possible. With it, nothing is impossible.

Mary McLeod Bethune

Don't pray when you feel like it. Have an appointment with the Lord.

Corrie ten Boom

Take a few moments today to reflect on how your image of God has changed through your life. What is the most helpful title, phrase or image for you?

 Pray today for what God wants from you rather than what you want from God.

 Remind yourself today that the only moment that matters is this one. Hand the past and the future over to God, and make this day count!

Create a mood board for prayer. Collect favourite images that help your understanding of the nature of God and place this in front of you as a focus for prayer.

 A prayer for the future
Lord, the days to come are known to you alone. May I embrace the joy and challenges that lie ahead, knowing that you are with me at every step. Amen.

 You are the guardian of your gifts and talents, given by God. Pray today for insight into how you might best use them in the service of others.

When engaging in meditation or silent prayer, seek a balance between relaxation and awareness.

 Scientific studies have proven that a prayer or meditation habit has a prolonged positive impact on the parts of the brain responsible for reducing anxiety and depression.

 If it's not possible to seek forgiveness from a person directly, consider sharing your burden in the form of prayer.

A prayer couched in the words of the soul is far more powerful than any ritual.

Paulo Coelho

A prayer in its simplest
definition is merely a wish
turned Godward.

Phillip Brooks

As you pray for yourself and a challenging situation, ask God to show you what might be learned from it.

 Consider your conversation with God as the ultimate in communication; no Wi-Fi or phone signal required, just an open and willing heart.

 A prayer to value others more
Help me, Lord, to recognise that I am here today because of the kind actions shown to me. Allow me to replicate this for those I meet today. Amen.

 Meditate with arms and legs uncrossed to promote a sense of grounding and to prevent cramp!

Who do you want to be? Spend time today praying for help in becoming your best self and how, as that person, you might grow in faith.

 Churches in medieval times were places of refuge or sanctuary for those in need. Where is your sanctuary or sacred space? Use this as a focus for meditation.

 Don't negate or diminish your feelings but recognise the perspective you can gain from remembering and praying for others bearing heavier burdens than your own.

As the clocks go back this month, commit to making good use of the extra hour in the service of others!

 A prayer for the lonely
Pour out your love today, Lord, on those who feel alone. I ask for your help in becoming a better companion and neighbour to those in need. Amen.

Halloween: Whilst children shriek and squeal at ghosts and witches, hand over to God in prayer those things you fear and from which you seek protection.

NOVEMBER

All Saints' Day: As a focus for your prayer today, remember those who have sacrificed their lives for their faith and for the lives of others.

A prayer for those who have died

I remember today those whom I have loved and lost. Welcome them into your kingdom and comfort those who mourn them. Amen.

Don't keep prayers to yourself. If you are praying for someone, let them know; it is likely to be a great comfort.

 At this time of remembering those who have gone before us, thank God for the blessings brought to you by a person who has died.

 Do you remember watching fireworks as a child? Moments of awe and wonder can be harder to find as we get older; pray that you will recognise WOW moments when they come along.

A prayer for arguments
Help me, Lord, to fight fair: to see fault in a person's behaviour rather than their character, and to resolve to explore our differences without causing hurt. Amen.

 As you wake this morning, pray for a person who has helped you recently, and commit to thanking them before you turn in tonight!

 We are immersed in a culture of entitlement. Today focus not on what you want but ask God instead for what you need.

Faith and prayer are
the vitamins for the
soul; man cannot live in
health without them.

Mahalia Jackson

In prayer it is better to have a heart without words than words without a heart.

John Bunyan

NOVEMBER

Armistice Day: I offer prayers today for those who have paid the ultimate price for freedom and peace. I ask God to comfort those who mourn those lost as a result of conflict around the world. Amen.

A prayer to see God in others
For those times when I am unable to see the good in another person, I ask you, Lord, to remind me that we are all made in your image and likeness. Amen.

If where you find yourself today is not where you want to be, ask God to point you in the right direction.

NOVEMBER

 14 Reflect today on your early experiences of prayer. Is there a person who showed you how to pray as a child? What can you learn from them and their example today?

 15 *A prayer for the impulsive*
As I rush through this day, Lord, help me to pause when making decisions and to take a breath when I am tempted to judge the actions of others. Amen.

 16 Religion is often used as an excuse for conflict, when many faith traditions have much in common. Pray today for greater understanding and open dialogue between different faiths.

Consider reading more about another faith tradition. You may be surprised by the common ground you share.

 As you pray today, reflect upon your dreams for the future. Is there anything you could do tomorrow to begin your journey towards one of them?

 A prayer to be God's presence in the world
Help me to remember, Lord, that I am here with a purpose; may I act as your hands and voice in the world. Amen.

Pray as though everything depended on God. Work as though everything depended on you.

St Augustine of Hippo

Our prayers run along one road and God's answers by another, and by and by they meet.

Adoniram Judson

God always allows you to begin again. Make today the day for a fresh start, trusting in God to provide you with what you need.

 It's tempting to try to bargain with God, making outlandish promises in exchange for an answered prayer. Try to focus instead on how your intention might fit into God's plan for you today.

 Focus on your breathing as you pray today. Take naturally slow and deep breaths as unwanted distractions are released from your mind.

NOVEMBER

 25 Many faith traditions have multiple names or images for God. Whilst we will never fathom the nature of God, it's only human to try.

 26 *A prayer when all seems lost*
For the times when I don't know what to do, I hand my troubles to God, trusting that God has the power to make all things new. Amen.

 27 A recent study suggests that adults spend more time engaged with technology than sleeping. Commit to spending more time unplugged from technology and plugged into your relationship with God and others.

Sit still, do nothing, wait and listen for God.

 A prayer for waiting
Lord, it can be so difficult to wait, whether we are fearful or joyful. Be with us in the waiting times. Amen.

 A prayer for the marginalised
I pray today for those who feel invisible in our society. I ask God's help in holding every person as equal as God does. Amen.

DECEMBER

World AIDS Day: Keep in mind those living with HIV/AIDS, those who care for them and those who are working towards a cure.

 Festivals of light throughout the world share a common theme: the victory of light over darkness as a symbol of good overcoming evil. Keep this image in mind as your prayer focus today.

 What last moved you to tears? When did you last feel goose bumps? Thank God today for the joy and wonder in your life.

DECEMBER

 Do you know the origin of your name? Do you share it with a religious person? Does it have a special meaning? What might this insight mean for you?

 A prayer for volunteers
I thank you, Lord, for the generosity of spirit shown by volunteers throughout the world. May I commit to using my skills in the service of others. Amen.

St Nicholas' Day: St Nicholas is the character upon which Father Christmas is based. Pray today for children in need of love and protection throughout the world.

The fewer the words, the better the prayer.

Martin Luther

The best and most
beautiful things in the
world cannot be seen or
even touched. They must
be felt with the heart.

Helen Keller

DECEMBER

 9 Remember today that no difficulty is greater than the power and love of God.

 10 Repetition of formal prayers can provide an opportunity for meditation and clarity of thought. Try repeating a prayer you know well and notice whether this brings you peace and contemplation.

 11 *A prayer for trust in God*
Lord, you know me better than I know myself. Help me to place all of my trust in you. Amen.

 12 This month seek ways to share your generous spirit with those in need.

DECEMBER

 Candles are a common symbol used in prayer in many faith traditions. The light represents triumph over darkness whilst the rising flame symbolises the prayer rising upwards to God.

 The ancient Celts used a circle prayer known as a *caim* to protect a person or situation. Think about what you would like kept within the circle.

 A prayer for children in conflict
God of compassion, watch over the children of our world living in conflict or under the threat of violence. May the innocence of childhood be always protected. Amen.

A world of social media and online living makes it easy to live several identities at the same time. Today, pray with the question, 'Who am I?'

 Meditate today on a situation that feels overwhelming. As you pray about it, to gain a sense of perspective imagine yourself zooming out and observing it from a distance.

 Remember in prayer those who will spend Christmas alone this year.

Ask, and it will be given
you; search, and you will
find; knock, and the door
will be opened for you.

Matthew's Gospel 7:7

Go placidly amidst the noise and haste and remember what peace there may be in silence.

Max Ehrmann

DECEMBER

 21 Take a break from the festive preparations to remember the joy you felt as a child at Christmas. If you can, share these memories with any excited children you might know.

 22 *A winter prayer*
I thank you, Lord, for the beauty of this season, for crisp blue skies and snowflakes, for the joy and expectation brought by the birth of Jesus. Amen.

 23 Before you are tempted to complain about how busy you are, pause to pray today for those who have no special meal to prepare or gifts to wrap this Christmas.

DECEMBER

 24 The commercial aspect of Christmas can be overwhelming. Spend a few moments today seeking God and remind yourself of the story of the first Christmas.

 25

Christmas Day: Light a candle in your home today and commit to saying a prayer of thanksgiving each time you pass it.

Remember in prayer today those who have to work over the holiday season.

 As you pray today, ask God to comfort those who have lost a loved one during the year.

 As you draw in a deep breath, imagine that, as you breathe out, God's spirit is collecting any worries or negative thoughts you may have.

A prayer for new ventures
As the year draws to an end, Lord, I ask for your blessing on any new ventures that next year holds for me. Amen.

 As a prayer focus today, spend time reflecting upon the highlights and challenges of the past year. Hand them over to God as moments of learning as the year comes to an end.

New Year's Eve: You are on a journey of faith which continues all the days of your life. Thank God today for the ways in which your life has been enriched this year by a more active prayer life.

If you're interested in finding out more about our books, find us on Facebook at **Summersdale Publishers** and follow us on Twitter at **@Summersdale**.

www.summersdale.com